EATING DISORDERS
Hope for Hungering Souls

Mark E. Shaw
with
Rachel Bailey and Bethany Spence

EATING DISORDERS
Hope for Hungering Souls

Mark E. Shaw
With Rachel Bailey and Bethany Spence

Copyright 2014
Scripture quotations are from The Holy Bible,
English Standard Version® (ESV®), Copyright © 2001
by Crossway, a publishing ministry of Good News Publishers.
Used by permission. All rights reserved.

Except for brief quotes, no part of this book
may be reproduced by any means
without written consent of the publisher.

Cover Design by Melanie Schmidt

ISBN: 978-1-936141-22-7

Printed in the United States of America

Focus Publishing
PO Box 665
Bemidji, MN 56619

TABLE OF CONTENTS

Foreword	1
Introduction	3
1. The Truth about Eating Disorders	15
2. Deception and Amputation	23
3. New Attitudes	39
4. Walking in Victory	59
5. A Triumphant Life	65
Conclusion	69
Appendix Worldly Words vs. God's Word	71

FOREWORD

Throughout most of history, women have internalized the world's message that in order to be "beautiful," they must be slender. In ancient times, throughout the medieval period and in the present day, women have fallen prey to the idol of thinness, and used self-destructive behavior to obtain it. Currently, eating disorders are on the rise in Eastern Europe and much of Asia. Although the terms became household words in the 1980's, anorexia and bulimia are not new practices, nor are they "American" behaviors. The prevalence of these enslaving behaviors and the mindset that fuels them are a universal phenomenon, which points back to the common sin nature that we all share.

Contrary to popular belief, eating disorders are *not* diseases. They are learned behaviors, which, by the grace of God, can be unlearned. The key to freedom from all life-dominating sin, including anorexia and bulimia, is in "being transformed by the renewing of [our] minds" (Romans 12:1). Authors Dr. Mark E. Shaw, Bethany Spence, and Rachel Bailey offer the reader real, lasting hope—which cannot be found in medication, psychotherapy, or blaming genetics, parents, or the media. Freedom is found in the Person and work of Jesus Christ. You will better understand your position in Christ, and how to apply biblical principles of change—deliberately "putting off" old habits of sin, and choosing to "put on" God-pleasing ones. Learning to reject the world's lies about beauty, the reader will come to understand true beauty as God defines it; to "set [your] mind on things above, rather than on earthly things" (Colossians 3:2); and ultimately walk out of the "pit" of an eating disorder into lasting freedom and joy in Christ.

Marie Notcheva
Author, *Redeemed from the Pit: Biblical Repentance and Restoration from the Bondage of Eating Disorders* (Calvary Press)
Certified counselor, Institute for Nouthetic Studies

Eating Disorders: Hope for Hungering Souls

INTRODUCTION

Eating Disorders, just like those who struggle with them, come in all shapes and sizes. There are the restrictive patterns that characterize Anorexia Nervosa. There are the seemingly uncontrollable and impulsive behaviors of binging and purging in Bulimia Nervosa. There is the excessive consumption of food with no regard to hunger cues called Binge Eating Disorder in the DSM-V[1]. Whether diagnosed or not, eating disorders run rampant in our culture; they are sometimes subtly and sometimes overtly promoted across store billboards, commercial clips, and personal profiles. Eating Disorders are unashamedly advertised in pictures coined "thinspirational." Radical weight loss strategies are normalized and exchanged on forums and in chat rooms. Scantily clad, ultra-skinny young women are on the covers of magazines with headlines that claim, "Lose 10 pounds in 10 days." The so-called "best" dieting tips are idolized via Facebook status updates. Witty Tweets reinforce the destructive patterns of those who refuse to eat, transforming starvation into an admirable demonstration of self-discipline. Eating disorders are everywhere; sample the statistics:

- According to Exercise Physiologist and ASU professor, Glenn Gaesser, **"over 50% of females surveyed between the ages of 18-25 would prefer to be run over by a truck than be fat, and 75% would rather be mean or stupid."**[2]
- A survey of middle-school children by the Journal of the American Dietetic Association found that **"81% of ten year olds are afraid of being fat."**[3]

---

[1] Diagnostic and Statistical Manual of Mental Disorders, Ed. 5; American Psychiatric Association, 2013.

[2] Glenn Gaessner, *Big Fat Lies: The Truth About Your Weight and Your Health* (New York: Fawcett Columbine, 1996), 28

[3] L. Mellin, S. McNutt, Y. Hu, G. B Schreiber, P. Crawford, and E. A Obarzanek., "A longitudinal study of the dietary practices of black and white girls 9 and 10 years old at enrollment: The NHLBI growth and health study" in *Journal of Adolescent Health* (1997) 20(1), 27-37.

- Research by The Renfrew Center Foundation for Eating Disorders proposes: **"Eating Disorders affect up to 24 million Americans and 70 million individuals worldwide."**[4]
- The Dove Global Beauty Study done in 2006 found that **"67% of women withdraw from life-engaging activities because they feel badly about their looks."**[5]
- **"Five to ten percent of anorexics die within ten years of onset, 18-20 percent die within twenty years of onset, and only 50 percent report ever being cured,"**[6] according to the National American Psychiatric Association.

I give thanks to you, O Lord my God, with my whole heart, and I will glorify your name forever (Psalm 86:12). As the psalmist says in this verse, our team's goal in writing this resource is to glorify God by demonstrating that His Word and His Spirit have much to say regarding so-called modern day problems. Even Christians sometimes forget to turn to God first in a moment of distress and are duped into believing that today's problems are beyond the body of Christ's realm of expertise. This is because issues have been repackaged and relabeled in such a manner as to not be specifically mentioned in the Bible. We want to point everyone to the Word of God for biblical solutions that are truly hopeful and helpful for modern day problems. We want God to be glorified by demonstrating that He provides answers in His Word and by His Spirit that cause transformational heart change.

---

[4] The Renfrew Foundation for Eating Disorders, *"Eating Disorders 101 Guide: A Summary of Issues, Statistics, and Resources"* (2006), Web. <http://www.renfrew.org>.

[5] N. Etcoff, S. Orgach, J. Scott, and H. D'Agostino, "Beyond Stereotypes: Rebuilding the Foundation of Beauty Beliefs" in *Dove Beauty Campaign Global Study* (2005), Web. January 14, 2014. <http://www.personal.psu.edu/axr15/courses/eMarketing2009/Dove%20Beyond%20Stereotypes%20White%20Paper.pdf>.

[6] American Psychiatric Association, *"Practice Guidelines for Eating Disorders"* in *American Journal of* Psychiatry (1993) 150 (2), 212-228.

Jesus Christ was all about heart change and that is evident in His teachings. When you read passages like the Sermon on the Mount in Matthew 5-7, clearly He emphasized inward, heart change that can only come through the power of the Holy Spirit working by grace through faith and repentance on a daily basis. While outward behaviors are important, they are simply a reflection of what is truly going on in a person's heart demonstrating what is valued, believed, and desired. The result of a changed heart is changed outward behavior. When we see a person change from the inside out, we know that God alone offered the power through the Holy Spirit to transform that heart; therefore, He alone receives the glory.

God brings the one-time event of salvation to a soul and then begins His work on a daily basis to bring sanctification (or spiritual growth) to that soul. God's Word and the Holy Spirit are required for sanctification just as faith and repentance are necessary, too. We share in the joy of knowing that He is working through us to be like spiritual tour guides: pointing people to the awesome sights of God's amazing works. Our prayer is that you would find hope and help as you look to God's Word and Spirit to transform your heart.

We recommend that you read this book with a trusted Christian friend who can disciple you. Our goal is not to merely share new information with you but to provide you an opportunity for training that transcends teaching. Teaching is wonderful, yet training is the key element of disciple-making that Jesus utilized with His disciples in teachable moments; that is, the direct application of the truth in the walk of life. At Vision of Hope, a residential facility for young women struggling with eating disorders, addictions of all types, unplanned pregnancy, and self-harm habits, we see that it is not information alone that changes the heart but training in a disciple-making relationship with another person that sets up the right environment for a young woman to know and walk with Christ.

With just these few statistics above, you can easily see that the problem of eating disorders and disordered eating is at epidemic proportions. Perhaps you can relate to some of the feelings of a person struggling with an eating disorder. Thankfully, there is real hope and practical help available in Jesus Christ: the only One who offers real solutions to hurting souls like Katie[7] who shares her experience through her diary.

Mark E. Shaw, D.Min., Executive Director

Vision of Hope
5652 Mercy Way
Lafayette, IN 47905
Telephone: (765) 447-5900
www.faithlafayette.org/voh

---

[7] Katie is a completely fictional character.

KATIE'S DIARY

January 5th

Dear Diary,

I've had it! I've tried everything to deal with this, but I just can't handle it anymore. The fights are too much. My dad is so hard on my mom; I hear her crying at night. It's breaking my heart! If that wasn't enough, my parents have been uber-weird toward me lately. They tell me they're worried I'm losing too much weight. I don't like the way they watch everything I eat (or don't eat)... and I don't really want to talk to them about it, anyway. My boyfriend, Josh, says I should just move out. I know we've only been seeing each other for a few months, but Josh really cares about me and he wants me to come live with him. He really listens to me, and often sacrifices time with his friends to spend time with me. I like a guy who puts me first. It's refreshing. Plus, he hasn't been pushy like other guys I know. Josh just kind of takes it slow and allows our love to develop naturally. I think he's a keeper! Anyway, I'm gonna start packing... I think Josh is right; it's time to get away from my parents and forge my own path, ya know?

XO, Katie

KATIE'S DIARY

March 17th

Dear Diary,

I'm so sick of feeling like this! I despise my body! I'm scared of losing Josh because of the way I look. I can't keep up this mask of "I'm ok" anymore . . . and once Josh finds out I'm crazy, he won't love me anymore. I've been doing pretty well at avoiding meals, but tonight Josh planned this "dinner for two" thing. He made Mac & Cheese (of course!) and it was DISGUSTING! Luckily, after dinner I was able to slip away and fix that little mistake. Josh doesn't know that I've been throwing up after I eat. I think I cover it pretty well. I've tried to stop for him. I've tried everything to be normal. It's ridiculous! I just want to be able to eat without having all this anxiety with every bite. At the same time, I'm scared to think what my body will do if I don't control what I eat.

XO, Katie

KATIE'S DIARY

May 12th

Dear Diary,

I purged today, not that it's noteworthy. It's more "normal" now than ever. I feel really cold and empty. I want to make some hot chocolate, but I haven't earned that today and don't want to give myself another reason to hate my life . . . I'm sure there are better things in life to worry about than this, but somehow this is the only thing that I can think about lately. I also bought a pair of pants today that are a bit too small. They're my motivation for losing weight.

XO, Katie

KATIE'S DIARY

July 6th

Dear Diary,

This is the worst my eating disorder has ever been! People tell me I'm too thin, but I feel 300 lbs. I can't get this heaviness off me! I am just purging and taking laxatives and I don't want to even go into it all . . . I hope and pray that I'm not going to get fat. To me, that's the worst thing in the world. Call me vain if you like—Christians do. That's another thing: I'm right at the verge of kicking God to the curb of my life. I don't think I can follow what the Bible says . . . it all seems like a fairy tale to me, an allegory that doesn't fit real life. If God really wants me to beat this and believe Him, He better give me the tools and motivation to start me off. I feel like a small child tugging at His shirt and saying "Daddy, help me!" He's waving me off with barely a glance my way, murmuring, "Later, honey, Daddy's busy right now." I just don't know how God's existence affects my life . . . I know it affects my death . . . To die, to escape this painful existence, is gain, right?

XO, Katie

KATIE'S DIARY

July 13th

Dear Diary,

I'm really considering ending it, right here, right now. No one's home; and no one would miss me anyway. My battles with food and self-degrading thoughts are my only and constant companions. Josh is seeing another girl (he thinks he's hiding it from me!) and my parents haven't really been in the picture since I left . . . My brother's texted me a few times about his life in the city, but he wouldn't notice too much if I didn't reply. He's too busy with his drug-dealing pals to miss me much; probably would be too high to remember me anyway. Suicide is the best option for me at this point. I don't want to disappoint everyone, but I don't want to keep living like this . . . Is there any hope left in this life for me?

XO, Katie

You Are Not Alone

Rejected. Alone. Undesirable. Homeless. Depressed. These are but a few of the words you could use to describe Katie. She is hungering for temporary things that will never provide permanent satiation. Perhaps these words could even describe you. Are you feeling rejected, alone, undesirable, homeless, or depressed? If so, you are not alone because there is another Person who fit into these categories and it may surprise you to find out who it is.

    The Bible says Jesus was rejected and alone (Matthew 13:57-58; 26:40), undesirable (Isaiah 53:2), homeless (Luke 9:58), and at times in great despair (Matthew 26:38, Luke 22:44). The Bible also tells you that your High Priest (Jesus) is able to identify with you in your weakness because He was tempted in every way just as you are, yet without sin (Hebrews 4:15). This brings us to an undeniable conclusion: God knows and He cares. He has felt the uncomfortable feeling of being alone, rejected by those He created in love. He has known great pain and sorrow. He has felt the weight of the harsh ridicule and judgments of those He loves and came to save. He knows stress. He has experienced what the world calls depression. He knows.

    Feeling the weight and depravity of humanity, and despite your sinful desires and choices, the holy, majestic God chose to love you unconditionally. He took on the form of a man to dwell with sinners on this depraved planet. After a short lifetime of healing the sick and blind, saving the tax collectors, and forgiving the prostitutes—all the while experiencing firsthand the darkness of our world—Jesus chose to follow through with His plan to save lost souls. He suffered an excruciating death at the hands of those whose heartbeat He Himself sustained, and His body was laid in a borrowed tomb. All seemed lost, but then three days later He rose up from the dead and continued to display His love for mankind until He ascended back into heaven. He did it all so that those who place their trust in Him for the forgiveness of their sins may dwell in His loving embrace forever one day. He knows, and He cares.

Introduction

Perhaps you're wondering "If God really knows and cares, where is He in my life? Why doesn't He intervene? Why is He so silent?" Maybe it's been a while since you've felt close to God. Maybe you never have. But did you know that God has given you His very words in written form so that you can hear from Him? These words are conveniently contained in one inerrant book, the Bible. God says that the Bible was literally breathed out by Him, and that through His power and the knowledge of who He is (found in His Word) He provides everything you need to live a godly, abundant life (2 Peter 1:3, John 10:10).

"But that's not true," you may be thinking, "the Bible doesn't talk about the things I'm dealing with. God says nothing about my struggles." Well, Friend, I am happy to tell you that when you use biblical language to define your problems, you will find biblical solutions. Let's explore together some of the issues that you may be dealing with, and see what the Bible has to say about them! In fact, we will look at four steps in the biblical process for change found in 2 Timothy 3:16 and Ephesians 4:20-24 of God's Word to apply His powerful truths to your heart's motives to bring about lasting transformation.

The Lord God created you with an insatiable hunger, but that hunger will never be satisfied by anything temporary on earth. That hunger will only be satisfied in a meaningful relationship with Him and with His body: the church. God has provided people who can come alongside you to disciple you so that you do not have to try to understand the Bible alone. You need teachers, encouragers, prayer-warriors, and instructors to truly change. They will point you to Christ and your personal relationship with Him.

When you take your eyes off of Him and look to what the world offers for satisfaction, you will hunger again, even as a Christian. Christ-followers must be completely dedicated to God and want only Jesus. Sometimes, a person wants a better life and while that is not always a wrong desire, God designed you to want Him because He knows it is best for you. In this book, it is our prayer that you become totally satisfied in your relationship with Christ.

Chapter One

The Truth About Eating Disorders

In the process of change, we start with Jesus, since the truth is in Him according to Ephesians 4:20-21: **But that is not the way you learned Christ!—assuming that you have heard about Him and were taught in Him, as the truth is in Jesus.** Even though you may have your doubts that change is possible and that it begins with Him, the truth is that transformation occurs when you learn about Who He is from the Word of God as 2 Timothy 3:16-17 says: **All scripture is given by inspiration of God, and is profitable for doctrine, for reproof, for correction, for instruction in righteousness: that the man of God may be perfect, thoroughly furnished unto all good works.**[8]

When something is profitable for us it means it is helpful, valuable and worthwhile. The Bible says that knowing God personally—and not just knowing facts about God—is vital to permanently changing your life for the better. The way you will grow in this intimate relationship with God is by reading the Bible, believing it by the power of the Holy Spirit, and then acting upon its truth whether you feel like it or not.

Change does not occur by being passive. "Letting go and letting God" is a nice idea with a shred of truth in it, but it is not found in Scripture. Instead, Philippians 2:12b-13 instructs a believer in Christ to **"work out your own salvation with**

---

[8] This one Bible reference is from the King James Version (KJV) because I prefer the word "doctrine" in that translation over "teaching" in the English Standard Version (ESV). Doctrine captures the idea of standards better than teaching does.

fear and trembling, for it is God who works in you, both to will and to work for his good pleasure." As a Christian struggling with what is called an eating disorder you can apply these verses to your life by carving out time in your schedule to pray, study the Word, meet with an accountability partner and trusted Christian friend, attend corporate worship services on Sundays, and serve the local church in some capacity. None of those items are passive at all; these are active choices you must begin to make in order to experience transformation.[9]

In the chart below, we have outlined the basic process of change according to the Bible. We parallel two passages of Scripture because of their consistency in the prescription for change. Both Ephesians 4:20-24 and 2 Timothy 3:16 lay out similar steps for transformation for a person struggling with an eating disorder. More details about each step in the process of change are found in the corresponding chapters. For now, all you must understand is that God is systematic in His approach with us in all problem areas of our lives. First, He wants to reveal the truth of our situation. This is only found in Jesus Christ and is our doctrine, or set of principles and standards. When we look to Jesus, we often see our own flaws and shortcomings which leads us to the second step of the put-off, or reproof. Jesus makes us aware of what attitudes, actions, and words we must rid ourselves of. The third step of correction, or being renewed in the spirit of your mind, is your opportunity to partner with the Holy Spirit. Now that you are aware of what you are doing incorrectly, you have a choice to make: continue believing the lies and living the way you have always lived OR correct your attitude with God's

---

[9] There is a hyper-sensitivity to "works" in Christianity and we agree that one cannot work to earn salvation. However, historical, biblical teachings of the church emphasize the synergistic partnership of a believer fueled through a working partnership with the Holy Spirit. In this sense, believers are called to be active in their faith by working out what they believe after salvation.

truth and live in a new way according to the Bible. The Holy Spirit enlightens your eyes with the first two steps, and will directly help you with this third and fourth step as you learned previously in Philippians 2:12b-13. Finally, the fourth step is the putting-on of new actions and behaviors which result from your changed attitude and opinions. These new actions will look a whole lot like Jesus to those around you which is God's goal for your transformation. God wants you to look less like you and more like Him in terms of your inward heart attitudes and character. (NOTE: We are not talking about looking like Jesus on the outside in a physical sense but only in a spiritual sense.)

Biblical Process for Change

	Step 1	Step 2	Step 3	Step 4
Ephesians 4:20-24	**Learned Christ (v. 20-21)**	Put-Off (v. 22)	Renewed in the Spirit of Your Mind (v. 23)	Put-On (v. 24)
2 Timothy 3:16	**Doctrine**	Reproof	Correction	Instruction in Righteousness
Explanation	**Standard set by your Creator found in His Word**	Falling short of that Standard, this is the part of your former life of sinful habits to be discarded	Holy Spirit provides power to transform with new attitude and new ability to please God	Practical application of righteousness of Christ that now meets God's standard!

Intimacy with the biblical God of love is a key ingredient to beginning the process of change because it assumes you are reading the Word to learn more of Christ. The chapter you are reading is designed to contrast how the world defines eating disorders with how God defines it so that you can walk in the light of truth. Imagine being in the dark late at night without any power to turn on the lights. That is what it is like for someone to overcome a powerful problem like an eating disorder without the Word of God. God does not want you living in the dark, which is why He sent His only begotten Son who became the Word made into flesh. Understand the significance of John 1:14: **And the Word became flesh and dwelt among us, and we have seen his glory, glory as of the only Son from the Father, full of grace and truth.** This verse refers to Jesus the Messiah who came to fulfill the Word of God perfectly and then to give His life freely in a violent death as a payment for our sins.

For those struggling with eating disorders, there are two voices to listen to but only one offers real hope. One is the world's voice; the other voice is God's. Both of these voices see the same problems, and describe them almost the same way; yet the two voices offer vastly different solutions. Here are some of the symptoms that you may be experiencing:[10]

- Feeling fat, regardless of actual weight
- Thinning hair
- Excessive exercise, even when tired or injured
- Loss of self-control when eating
- Vomiting, laxative, or exercise abuse
- Overeating or restricting food in response to stress
- Frequent fluctuations in weight
- Eating large amounts of food when not physically hungry

---

[10] The Renfrew Center Foundation for Eating Disorders, *"Eating Disorders: Signs and Symptoms,"* Web. Accessed January 22, 2014. <http://renfrewcenter.com/sites/default/files/Signs%20and%20Symptoms.pdf>.

- Turning to food as a way of coping with feelings
- Eating to the point of feeling uncomfortably full
- Eating alone because of shame or embarrassment
- Showing signs of depression and withdrawal
- Extreme feelings of guilt and shame after eating

What the world cannot offer in its solution is God's power. God's solution requires divine power in a "divine intervention" that transforms the desires of the heart, leading to changes in behavior. That intervention is possible as the Holy Spirit works in partnership with your obedience to the Word of God. In other words, you will be required to do your part to follow God's commands, while completely relying upon the Holy Spirit for empowerment (Philippians 2:12-13).

Here's the good news: when you do your part, God is faithful to do His work. Here's even better news: when you fail to do your part, God is faithful and His love for you will not change once you are His adopted child. You can count on Him even when you fail. Failing may not provide the successful fruit you desire from the consequences of wrong choices, but that does not change the reality of God's unchanging love for you. God is gracious, loving, and powerful to work His plan for your life for His own glory (Ephesians 2:10). For this reason, be encouraged knowing God will empower you to think differently about your problem and to execute His plan for your spiritual growth because ultimately it glorifies Him, and He wants to be glorified through your life. Give God your best efforts because He deserves nothing else. Learn more about Jesus Christ and His standards and doctrine from His Word.

The World vs. The Word

Now, let's contrast what the world says about some of the issues you may be struggling with versus what God says about depression, eating disorders, and addictions.

Depression

Depression has become a very common occurrence in society. The word "depression" is used to describe a state of hopelessness, deep sorrow, lack of energy or incentive, dejection, and the like. As you witnessed in Katie's story, these feelings can also lead to suicidal thinking. The Bible labels these thoughts and feelings *despair*. Genesis 4 says Cain's face became *downcast* when he saw that his brother's offering had been accepted by God, when his own had not. In another biblical account, Jonah experienced *despair* to the point of wishing to die (Jonah 4). Even King David, whom the Bible says was "a man after God's own heart," experienced great *despair* as he expressed in Psalm 13. And despair isn't always sinful. Jesus experienced deep sadness to the point of sweating drops of blood in Matthew 26:38 and Luke 22:44. You can know without a doubt that Jesus was completely sinless; therefore, there are appropriate times to grieve, be sad, and downcast. There is much to cry about in our fallen, sinful world. Yet despair becomes sinful when your heart desires are displeasing to the Lord by being saddened when He is not. Our thoughts, emotions, and behaviors must match God's in the sense that you learn to think as He does, as is revealed in His Word. Once again, this is why you start with Jesus in the process of biblical change because you want to know Him and what He says.

Eating Disorders

You will not find the words *eating disorder* in the Bible but that does not mean that the Word of God is silent about this issue. The real issue begins by understanding that God is your Creator and you belong to Him. He expects you to be a good steward of what He has given you, and your body is no exception. It is easy to think that your body is yours to shape and form how you want it to be, but in reality God has fearfully and wonderfully created your body for the sole purpose of glorifying Him. In 1 Corinthians 6:19-20, it says: **Or do you not know that your body is a temple of the Holy Spirit within you, whom you have from God? You are not your own, for you were bought with a price. So glorify God in your body.** The word "glorify" here means "to show God's character in your body."[11] In everything we do we are to be showing God's character to the world, and starving, binging, and purging are not Christ-like behaviors in a number of ways.

Paul teaches that you are to present your bodies as living sacrifices to God in Romans 12:1. You are told to glorify God in your eating and drinking and in every other way (1 Corinthians 10:31). The Bible also speaks strongly about gluttonous behaviors in passages such as Proverbs 23:20-21, Philippians 3:18-19, and Psalm 78:18 to name a few. For these reasons, consider an *eating disorder* by what the Bible would call it: poor stewardship of the body that ultimately belongs to Him. When we use the term eating disorder in this resource, we are referring to poor stewardship of the body.

Addictions

Biblically, an addiction is a life-dominating habit that enslaves its participant who willingly chooses to partake in the temporary pleasure. Individuals can become addicted to many things like TV, video games, drugs, alcohol, and even eating disorder behaviors like binging, purging, or starving. Strangely, you can begin to enjoy the binging and purging cycle or enjoy starving yourself. It becomes pleasurable in what it produces, a more desirable *skinny* body for example, though it is destructive in the end.

---

[11] Ryrie, Charles, *Ryrie Study Bible ESV,* Chicago, IL: Moody Publishers, 2011, p. 1398.

Addictions can take many forms, and all cause you to feel powerless to resist. The Bible calls these habits *enslaving sins* stemming from an idolatrous heart. You are cautioned in 1 Corinthians 6:12 to have boundaries so as to not become enslaved by anything. You are encouraged in John 16:33, Romans 6:6-7, 14, and all throughout the Bible that because Christ has defeated sin and overcome the world, you can be free from enslaving sins through Him.

Summary

God knows you and He cares for you as evidenced by His sending of His only Son to die in your place. Because of this caring love, God has graciously provided His Word as a guide to overcome any struggles in which you may find yourself, including what the world calls an addictive eating disorder. No problem is too big for Him, no person beyond His reach. You are not too far gone. God is not done with you; He has not forgotten you because He created you with a noble purpose: to live in a way that you glorify Him so that the world may know that He is worthy of all praise.

Your job is to learn all about Jesus from His Word and from someone discipling, or training, you. You are to be faithful to apply what you are learning about Jesus to your own life. Persevere, keep reading, and discover the deep and abiding freedom that Christ offers to you once and for all when you submit to His Word rather than to your own ideas or worldly philosophies as Isaiah 55:8-9 states:

> **For my thoughts are not your thoughts, neither are your ways my ways, declares the Lord. For as the heavens are higher than the earth, so are my ways higher than your ways and my thoughts than your thoughts.**

Chapter Two
Deception and Amputation

You cannot begin a journey without taking that first step. In the previous chapter, you discovered that learning about Jesus is just the beginning of the process of transformation because it increases your awareness of God's standards and doctrine. God clearly outlined in Ephesians 4:22 the second step in the process of change: **to put off your old self, which belongs to your former manner of life and is corrupt through deceitful desires.** 2 Timothy 3:16 refers to this part of the process as a *reproof* meaning "a correction from a fault."[12] The Bible presupposes that all persons are sinful from birth and in need of change. Even Christians need to change. Becoming a born again Christian means that you are free from the power and penalty of sin, but not its presence. Sin is present in all believers, which is why you need to be sanctified, cleansed from all unrighteousness, in a progressive process for the rest of your life. But God is faithful and He will do this work inside of you (Ephesians 2:10).

Biblical Process for Change

	Step 1	**Step 2**	Step 3	Step 4
Ephesians 4:20-24	Learned Christ (v. 20-21)	**Put-Off (v. 22)**	Renewed in the Spirit of Your Mind (v. 23)	Put-On (v. 24)

---

[12] Shaw, Mark. *The Heart of Addiction*. Focus Publishing, Bemidji, MN, 2008, p.28.

2 Timothy 3:16	Doctrine	**Reproof**	Correction	Instruction in Righteousness
Explanation	Standard set by your Creator found in His Word	**Falling short of that Standard, this is the part of your former life of sinful habits to be discarded**	Holy Spirit provides power to transform with new attitude and new ability to please God	Practical application of righteousness of Christ that now meets God's standard!

If you are a believer in Christ, you are faced with a dilemma: you are born again of the Holy Spirit (John 3:3) yet battle your old self, corrupted through deceitful desires (flesh). This war between the Spirit and the flesh is honestly acknowledged in the Bible in Galatians 5:13-18:

> **For you were called to freedom, brothers. Only do not use your freedom as an opportunity for the flesh, but through love serve one another. For the whole law is fulfilled in one word: "You shall love your neighbor as yourself." But if you bite and devour one another, watch out that you are not consumed by one another. But I say, walk by the Spirit, and you will not gratify the desires of the flesh. For the desires of the flesh are against the Spirit, and the desires of the Spirit are against the flesh, for these are opposed to each other, to keep you from doing**

the things you want to do. But if you are led by the Spirit, you are not under the law.

The battle between your flesh and the Holy Spirit begins with putting off your old self and not allowing yourself provisions to fulfill your corrupted desires.

While surrender is important in the transformation process, it is not without personal responsibility. Again, "letting go and letting God" often results in a passive acceptance of the way things are, often called *quietism*. After you are saved, you are called to think, speak, and act like Christ. This is different from the way you formerly thought, spoke, and acted. It is a fight. If you continue to be enslaved by habitual sin problems, you either do not yet understand the biblical process of change and the power given to you by God; or you are not truly born again. In this chapter, you will learn some of the hard self-deceptive truths about yourself, and the lies you believe that God by His grace wants you to replace. You will also identify some of the ways you must radically amputate opportunities to sin from your lifestyle. These are commands, not options for you, if you are a believer. You belong to the Creator and exist for the purpose of pointing other people to Jesus.

Self-Deception

Once upon a time, as the story begins, God creates the universe. In this world of perfect community, perfect order, and perfect inhabitants, God places His crowning creation: Adam and Eve. He puts Adam and Eve in the Garden to tend it and use it for good. Adam and Eve are free to fulfill this mandate however they see fit. Their only caveat is one fruit on one tree: **You must not eat of it lest you surely die***, God informs His children (Genesis 2:16-17). He knows it will be hard, but best, for Adam and Eve to trust Him.*

The next character slithers onto the scene, ready to enact a sinister plot. Through sweet talk and deception, Satan convinces Eve to believe the lie that God is not good and is holding out on her (1 Timothy 2:14). What started out as a tiny twist of the truth creates the most devastating choice in human history: Adam and Eve willfully disobey God's Word by eating the fruit from the forbidden tree. In believing a lie rather than the Truth, Adam and Eve are covered in shame and separated from their Creator, God. Lest we give Satan too much credit, remember that he only tempted Adam and Eve to do what they already wanted to do: trust themselves more than God.

The fall of humanity in Genesis 3 helps you understand why you lie to yourself, God, and others. Yet, it does not numb your conscience. More often than not, you feel guilty when you lie, and that is by God's grace. Yes, conviction (the Bible's term for the good kind of guilt) is part of God's grace and kindness because it leads you to repentance (Romans 2:4). Sin is not God's best for His creation, and it is His grace that shows you how sinful you are, leading you to freedom through the truth.

You knew at a very young age that it is wrong to lie, yet the question stands, *why do you lie?* Stated reflexively, *why should you tell the truth, especially when it is in your best interest to lie?* To answer the first question (*why do you lie?*) understand that Satan lied first. This wasn't hard for Satan to do. The Bible says that when Satan lies, he speaks his native tongue. Satan is devoid of truth and is labeled as the father of lies by Jesus (John 8:44). Add to this Satan's desire to separate you from God. That was his aim in the Garden of Eden, and that's his aim for all people today. The Bible describes Satan as going to God and accusing people of various things (Revelation 12:10; Zechariah 3:1). Just think: Satan, an infamous liar, is bringing up your case to God. This is why you need an advocate: Jesus Christ.

As the father of lies, it is Satan's great pleasure to influence *you* toward lying and deceit. Satan knows that lying is an abomination to God and will not go unpunished. Proverbs 19:5 says: **A false witness will not go unpunished, and he who breathes out lies will not escape.** In Psalm 101:7 God personally tells us: **"No one who practices deceit shall dwell in My house; no one who utters lies shall continue before My eyes."** These sobering verses are not meant to discourage or frighten you. They are meant to show you that lying to yourself, God, and others is a serious and devastating decision bringing separation in your relationship with God. Though Christians will never be separated from the love of Christ, it is possible to feel like you are far from God when you are mired in a pit of deception, lying, and sin. God does not want you to stay in that pit.

Lying is often motivated by fear. You may fear lots of things: what people think about you, what might happen in the future, what you have done in the past, and much more. Though it may be hard to see at first, it is pride and prideful thinking that permeate the liar's mind. That is why the lies must be identified and put-off, or discarded immediately. You cannot allow yourself to operate in self-deception, and you need trusted Christian friends in your life to speak the truth in love to you.

To answer the second question (*why should you tell the truth?*), remember that all persons are created for a purpose. When you fulfill this purpose, you experience more joy than you know what to do with. The temptation, though, is to trade joy that comes from long-term obedience for a momentary wisp of happiness. Living in this way leads to a never ending cycle of pursuing satisfaction that never permanently satisfies. The world calls this cycle "addiction"; the Bible calls it sinful idolatry.

God has intended and prescribed how He wants humans to act and it is in pursuit of knowing Him. He has created you to have a true identity in Christ. Anything else apart from God's intended purpose would be considered fraudulent living: a false identity. People often pursue an identity in any number of things like clothing, tattoos, hairstyles, shoes, bags, careers, acceptance, romantic relationships, athletic bodies, shapely figures, good food, and much more. The list is endless.

Identity and purpose can be found only in Christ, and there are two passages you can examine to help understand your purpose. The first is 2 Corinthians 5:9: **We make it our aim to please him.** The second verse is Romans 8:28-29: **And we know that for those who love God all things work together for good for those who are called according to his purpose . . . to be conformed to the image of his Son.** These two verses clearly describe God's intent for humanity: your goal must be to please Him first. In other words, you are to do the things that He delights in, and by so doing you will please Him. Again, you discover what these things are by reading His Word, the Bible. By accomplishing the goal of pleasing Him, you will become like Christ. You will be conformed, or shaped, spiritually-speaking, into the image of His Son.

In the above verses, the *good* that God is accomplishing in your life is that you would look more like Jesus in your thoughts, words, and actions. It begins by putting-off your old ways of thinking, speaking, and acting because they are corrupted and deceitful. In other words, they will ruin you and trick you to disobey Christ if you do not recognize them as lies and discard them quickly from your life (Eph. 4:22). God must reprove you and convict you by the Holy Spirit so that you know what is sinful in your heart. Conviction will show you what is in need of amputation. This means that even though the experience might be bad or painful from your perspective, it is ultimately God's perfect medium for transforming you. God transforms you from sad to joyful, from anxious to peaceful, from angry to gentle, from hateful to loving, from impulsive to self-controlled, from chaotic to faithful, and so on (Galatians 5:22-23).

Identifying the lies you believe is one way to partner with the Holy Spirit in looking more like Christ. Once identified, these lies are exposed in the light of God's Word through confession, or agreement with God. Good biblical counselors do not promote confession alone. Proverbs 28:13 gives us the next step after confession for discovering the mercy of God: **Whoever conceals his transgressions will not prosper, but he who confesses and forsakes them will obtain mercy.** Forsaking sin is the action step of repentance. Insight about sin is great, but you need to be moving toward change.

The Apostle Paul's challenge to the church at Corinth in 2 Corinthians 10:5 is to be violent toward your thoughts when they are sinful lies embedded in the old nature: **demolish arguments and every pretension that sets itself up against the knowledge of God, and take captive every thought to make it obedient to Christ.** One reason Paul uses the analogy of battle when he describes transforming your deceiving thoughts into truth is because lies are often discovered to be distortions of truth rather than outright falsehoods. In other words, lies are so deceptive to you because there is often some truth in the mixture of thoughts you are embracing, thoughts that are holding you captive.

The lies you believe will not appear to you willingly, rather, they will fight back, and they will hide. You must arm and ready yourself to confront them. This confrontation involves a radical behavior change called *amputation*. Living in truth involves a change of heart. Your goal cannot be to simply cut out negative behaviors, although this is important. God's Word teaches that your Savior wants your heart. He can see into the desires and motivations of your heart (Hebrews 4:12), and He wants your heart to be a reflection of His.

When the Bible uses the word "heart," it is not speaking of the physical organ that pumps blood. Instead, it is speaking about your inner person; your thoughts, motives, and desires. It is referring to what you want the most in life. The heart is the "control center" of the body. According to the Bible, everything you say or do comes from something in your heart (Luke 6:45, Proverbs 4:23). Your heart is prone to worship and to live for someone. In those moments when enslaved to an idolatrous passion, you are worshipping yourself and living to please yourself alone. Instead, you want your heart to worship and live for Christ alone.

Since everything you do flows from the condition of your heart, it is important to examine your heart for any presence of deceit. The following is a sampling of typical lies and distortions embedded in the hearts of people commonly plagued with destructive eating habits:

1) **Beauty**: *I am only as valuable as I am beautiful. Beauty equals happiness. No one will like me if I'm ugly. I won't get married unless my body is up to par. Skinny = Happy. Beautiful people always get what they want.*
2) **Perfectionism and Performance**: *Failure is ugly and unacceptable. Failure displeases God. Other people*

may fail, but that's not an option for me. I must appear to have everything together. I must be perfect.

3) **Control**: *Everything in my life is falling apart. I need to control my weight, my food intake, a number on a scale, etc. . . . I can't control my weight, my food intake, my fitness, my body, etc.*

4) **Pain/Suffering**: *I cannot stand this much pain. I must avoid hard things. I cannot go through that again.*

5) **Purpose**: *My goal in life is to take up as little space as possible. My goal in life is to be prettier than my sister. My goal in life is to have a boyfriend/get married. My goal in life is to never get fat.*

6) **Food/Calories**: *Food is my enemy. Food can only be eaten in certain circumstances and in certain ways. I cannot eat anything sweet. Everything I consume must be taken into account and logged. Consumption must be compensated for to prevent weight gain.*

7) **Health/Weight**: *I am not healthy until I weigh ____ pounds. They (doctors, friends, parents, etc.) can't tell me what is and isn't a healthy weight. My body is not healthy if I'm fat.*

8) **Exercise**: *Exercise is my primary tool against the battle of weight gain. Exercise must be performed in relation to how much I eat. Exercise is not exercise without pain/discomfort (I'm not pushing myself hard enough if . . .). Exercise is not a choice, but a necessity.*

9) **Self-imposed Rules**: *If I just follow my own set of rules, I won't get fat and others will accept me. If I eat a cookie, I just need to work-out twice as long today to make up for it.*

10) **People-pleasing**: *Others will not like me unless I am beautiful. I need to look a certain way for them to accept me.*

You may find yourself relating to some of these lies. As part of your transformation process, create your own list alongside those offered here. Begin your own process of identifying the lies you tend to believe. For now, this list is simply introducing the lies; you'll learn how to replace these lies with the truth of God's Word in later chapters. Now that you have learned about the importance of truth in replacing lies to be put-off, you will learn about the importance of *radical amputation*.

Radical Amputation

Radical amputation is a concept about which many people are apprehensive. Simply the word *amputation* suggests a difficult and uncomfortable experience, but what many Christians do not realize is that within this commitment is found the greatest freedom and joy. The process is similar to surgery for a diseased kidney that must be amputated in order for a person to live more abundantly. The surgical process hurts in the short-term yet in time, as the patient heals, strength returns so that there is long-term health. Jesus stated in Luke 9:23: **Whoever wants to be My disciple must deny themselves and take up their cross daily and follow Me.** John also made a similar statement in 1 John 2:6: **Whoever claims to live in Him must live as Jesus did.** Jesus Christ lived a life of radical love and self-denial. He is calling you to do the same.

Understanding radical amputation begins with Jesus who taught the truth in Matthew 5:29-30:

> **If your right eye causes you to stumble, gouge it out and throw it away. It is better for you to lose one part of your body than for your whole body to be thrown into hell. And if your right hand causes you to stumble, cut it off**

> **and throw it away. It is better for you to lose one part of your body than for your whole body to go into hell.**

Jesus was not speaking of physical amputation of actual parts of the body; rather, He was speaking metaphorically about radically amputating the things by which you are tempted to sin from within yourself. It is so important to identify what in your life is making it easier for you to sin. Once these obstacles are identified, they must be cut out! This is what Jesus is calling you to do—knowing that by following this principle you will find the greatest freedom and joy.

There is no middle ground in your decision to follow Jesus; no neutral. You're either fully committed, or not at all. The Bible teaches that you are known by your fruits: you are known as a true believer by demonstrating the Gospel (Matthew 7:15-16). You may claim to love Jesus, but if you are not obeying what the Word of God says then you are not showing that love. It is important to settle once and for all if you truly do love the Lord with all your heart, soul, mind, and strength (John 14:15; Luke 10:27). James 1:22-25 sums it up well:

> **But be doers of the word, and not hearers only, deceiving yourselves. For if anyone is a hearer of the word and not a doer, he is like a man who looks intently at his natural face in a mirror. For he looks at himself and goes away and at once forgets what he was like. But the one who looks into the perfect law, the law of liberty, and perseveres, being no hearer who forgets but a doer who acts, he will be blessed in his doing.**

Consider for a moment what happens when you get up in the morning. You go to the restroom and look in the mirror. What are you looking for? Disheveled hair, blemishes, and general imperfections, to name a few. What if you looked in the mirror and saw that your hair had matted into a rat's nest on top of your head? Would you shrug your shoulders and go to your workplace without touching it? No, you would take the time to fix the problem you saw in the mirror.

Suppose you were going on a date. Would you walk out the door and go to the fancy restaurant as-is, or would you take the time to look in the mirror and fix what is misplaced? These are exactly the kind of things James is commanding you to consider. The Bible is a mirror for your spiritual life. You look into it like a mirror to see what is wrong or misplaced. Then you act! As a believer, you are preparing to meet the Lord some day when either you die, or He comes back to take you to heaven. At that time, you will be face-to-face with the One who loves you so much that He suffered agony so that you could be with Him. This is so much greater than any "date" you could have here on earth. Because of this, you are to be making yourself look more and more like Jesus because you love Him and want to hear Him say the gentle words of Matthew 25:21: **"Well done, good and faithful servant."**

What I have just described to you is the *radical* part of the equation. Now, let us dive into the *amputation* aspect. As you look into the mirror of God's Word, you will see areas in which you need to adjust your thinking, change your behaviors, or perform an amputation altogether. Take bulimia and binge eating, for example. Many who struggle with periods of binge eating, whether followed by a purge or not, have certain foods with which they are tempted the most. These are sometimes called "binge foods" or "trigger foods." Have you considered making these particular foods absolutely off-limits to you?

Does this concept frighten you? Perhaps you are just the opposite, denying yourself food altogether. Are you willing to give up this pattern of living?

We were all made to worship the One true God, and when we are placing things in front of Him, we are essentially placing our faith and trust in those temporal, silly things. A good rule of thumb in figuring out if something has become an idol to you is by asking yourself these two questions: *Am I willing to sin in order to get this?* And *Do I react in a sinful way when I do not get this?* If the answer to either of these is yes, then that object, habit, or lifestyle has become like an idol to you. Take a moment to prayerfully consider the radical option of completely cutting these idolatrous desires out of your life.

For some of you, this may look like giving up your favorite restaurants or "thinspirational" websites. For others of you, this may mean making a healthy eating schedule and sticking to it, no matter how you feel or are tempted. But again, God doesn't want you to merely change your behavior. Our Lord looks at your thoughts and desires, and these should line up to look like Jesus. So as you are evaluating your struggle, look beyond your behaviors and into the motives behind them. Why are you participating in those behaviors? What are you so desiring from what enslaves you that you are willing to sin to get it? Know that any pleasure or fulfilled desire you receive from anything other than God is a cheap substitute. Why chase after the temporary and deceiving joys of food or a certain body weight when you can have the deep, abiding, eternal joy found in our Savior?

It is time to act on what God is revealing about your heart. Which areas need improvement? In which areas do you need to repent? What needs to be cut out altogether? Take a moment now to make a list of the things which have become an idol to you. Pray to the Lord for forgiveness, and repent! Your goal in life is to be pleasing to God and look more and more like Jesus; not simply in behavior, but in heart motives as well. Start now by repenting, and keep reading to learn how Jesus wants you to live in victory!

KATIE'S DIARY

October 19th

Dear Diary,

Since I last wrote, I've been getting help from a biblical counselor. She has really poured her heart and time into me (and I needed it!). It's a long story how I stumbled into her office.... And I really just wanted to talk about my suicidal tendencies, not my eating disorder. I thought all I needed was a new strategy. She helped me see I needed heart surgery (spiritually speaking, that is). I realize now that my eating disorder is not the main problem; I'm the main problem! I know that might sound cryptic, but I really believe it's true! I don't mean that I need to kill myself to kill my eating disorder, but in a sense I kind of do. What I mean is, I've got to kill all the old ways I used to think. I've got to kill all the old habits I used to turn to. I've got to kill all the desires I naturally want more than God.

I didn't get it at first, but my biblical counselor is patient with me. I realize that because I've been so deceived for so long, the truth sometimes doesn't "click" at first. That's why I have to diligently soak in and search out God's Word. I want my truth to be God's Truth. This attitude has really been impacting my outlook on life, so far! I haven't felt this joyful in awhile ... I'm hopeful it will stick around.

XO, Katie

Chapter Three
New Attitudes

If you are battling your struggles in your own strength, then you are failing. God wants you to allow Him to work through you: think of it as a partnership between you and God. God wants to give you His strength to fight the good fight. You cannot win this war with your limited resources. You need more. You need Him and His resources. Ephesians 4:23 is what you might call the *Holy Spirit step* in the process of change because it says this: **. . . and to be renewed in the spirit of your minds.** This third step simply means that God transforms your heart's desires to hate what you once loved by loving what you once hated. Only God by His Spirit working with the truth of His Word can bring about this attitude change in your heart. When this happens, it is called *repentance* and it is a gift from God (Ephesians 2:8-9; Romans 2:4).

2 Timothy 3:16 refers to this part of the change process as **correction.** It is time to choose to believe in truth rather than what you may have believed prior to learning what God's Word says about the issue. In this chapter, you will learn how walking in truth leads to a renewed mind. You will also recognize the importance of speaking the truth in love in identifying lies and replacing them with what God says. You will learn how replacing lies with the truth leads to a renewed mind.

Biblical Process for Change

	Step 1	Step 2	Step 3	Step 4
Ephesians 4:20-24	Learned Christ (v. 20-21)	Put-Off (v. 22)	**Renewed in the Spirit of Your Mind (v. 23)**	Put-On (v. 24)
2 Timothy 3:16	Doctrine	Reproof	**Correction**	Instruction in Righteousness
Explanation	Standard set by your Creator found in His Word	Falling short of that Standard, this is the part of your former life of sinful habits to be discarded	**Holy Spirit provides power to transform with new attitude and new ability to please God**	Practical application of righteousness of Christ that now meets God's standard!

Walking in Truth

  The mind can be a dangerous place where lies and sin stand ready to enslave. People often focus greatly on the sinfulness of negative behaviors, and forget where the battle begins. The reality is that you do most of your sinning in your mind. James says that you are tempted when you are drawn away and enticed **by your own desires** (James 1:14). Where do those desires originate? Do they not begin with a thought? You sin when you *think* that something will satisfy you outside of Christ or in addition to Christ. In this decision, you devote yourself to the belief that Christ is not sufficient. Consider the last time you sinned. No one would have to think back very far. What was the process that led to the sin? 1) You had a desire in your heart that 2) birthed into a thought that you 3) chose to believe. For some this may have been, "I will be happy once I am thinner." For others, perhaps it was more like, "I've already screwed up today, so I may as well keep going." There are endless possibilities of the thoughts that lead to sin, but a few things are certain: sin originates in your heart, later expressing itself in your thoughts. Therefore, your mind is in dire need of renewal!

When the Bible speaks of renewing the mind, it is not simply talking about thinking positively. If it were that simple, there would be a lot less people chained in bondage to sinful habits. Remember that 2 Corinthians 10:5 says: **We demolish arguments and every pretension that sets itself up against the knowledge of God, and we take captive every thought to make it obedient to Christ.** Based upon this verse, you are responsible to control your thoughts in such a way that they begin to be Christ-like. This means that you are actively and frequently asking yourself, "Is what I'm thinking about right now pleasing to God? Does it reflect His character? Would I be ashamed if someone else could hear my thoughts right now?" Questions such as these help you evaluate whether or not a thought should stay or go.

Consider the power of living out Philippians 4:8 in terms of mind renewal: **Finally, brothers and sisters, whatever is true, whatever is noble, whatever is right, whatever is pure, whatever is lovely, whatever is admirable—if anything is excellent or praiseworthy—think about such things.** When you are trying to improve your thought life, a good place to start is by evaluating your thoughts through the grid of Philippians 4:8. When you have a thought you are unsure of, stop and ask yourself, "Is this thought true?" If it is absolutely true according to the Word of God – not your own opinion or perception – then it may proceed to the next question: "Is this thought noble?" and so on. The diagram below, taken from Elyse Fitzpatrick's book *Love to Eat, Hate to Eat*, beautifully demonstrates this concept:

WORD	DEFINITION	ASK YOURSELF: *Is this thought...*
True	Factual	... *true to the facts, or am I exaggerating or ignoring them? Is it true to the facts that I know about God? His Word? His work? His purpose for me?*
Honorable	Esteemed	... *something that is beneath me as a daughter of the King? Does it keep my Father's kingship in sight?*
Right	Righteous	... *reflective of the righteousness that Christ purchased for me? Or is it part of the way that I thought before I knew His love?*
Pure	Clean	... *something I would be ashamed about if others knew I was entertaining it? Does it live up to God's standards of purity and holiness?*
Lovely	Winsome	... *something that would draw others to Christ? Is it sweet or bitter, beautiful or ugly?*
Good Repute	Attractive	... *a faith-filled assessment of the situation, or does it send my heart trembling in fear away from the Lord?*
Moral Excellence	Virtue	... *overflowing with the excellencies of Christ? Does it acknowledge His great love, mercy, grace, and holiness?*
Praiseworthy	Admirable	... *something that would cause others to praise God if they heard it? Does it cause my heart to be filled with thanks and worship?*

As you move through the grid of Philippians 4:8, if the answer to any of the questions is no—or if you are unsure—then that thought must not be allowed to stay. It must not be entertained in your mind. You must refuse to think on it because, according to Philippians 4:8, that thought is not fitting for a child of God. But remember this: you must not simply do away with ungodly thoughts, but must also work to replace them with godly ones. Determine to investigate what the Bible says about your most dominating thoughts, and choose to think on the truth that you find.

Now, zero in on the first aspect of the grid: truth. The Bible teaches that God and His Word are truth (John 1:17-18, John 14:6). If Christ's very character is truth, then in order to become more like Him you must not allow yourself to believe lies. It is possible to become so accustomed to filling your mind with deceitful lies that you no longer recognize when you are doing it! Your mind can be so clouded with what you perceive to be right that you no longer acknowledge truth at all. You must beg God to reveal to you the lies you tend to believe, and seek to demolish them!

Take another look at the common lies people believe in chapter 2. Perhaps one of the most prominent struggles in the area of stewardship is setting up unbiblical standards. Those who struggle with eating disorders tend to believe something bad will happen if they violate one of these standards. For example, you may have the standard that you must never be bigger than a certain size, weight, or certain person. Or perhaps you have determined that you will never eat in front of anyone. The possibilities are endless, and all are ways to worship idols of the heart.

Some people have an intricate grid of self-imposed rules and standards that they have set up as "truth" when they are not. For example, you may struggle with thinking, "I have to be the skinniest person in the room." Or "If I eat dessert, I will skip dinner." Or "If I eat dessert, I will simply purge in the bathroom and no one will know." Counselors are often amazed at the detailed set of rules beneath the surface of someone struggling with eating disorder behavior. If this is your struggle, you must open up to a trusted Christian friend immediately and unearth the rules you are following. To elevate self-imposed rules to the level of God's standards in His Word is called *legalism* and it is deadly. Often these attitudes are judgmentally imposed onto others, too, which is sometimes a cause of the death of relationships.

God has set up standards that are very good for you, and following these standards pleases and honors Him. By setting up standards of your own, you are essentially creating commandments for your own gods—or heart idols—that you have chosen to worship. You may have created many "Thou shalt not" statements that are absent from the pages of God's Word. Following such standards demonstrates total devotion to something other than God. It can be easy to believe that happiness will come when you measure up to these self-created commandments, but this is simply untrue. You may think that you feel better when you hold fast to your own commandments, but the reality is that your loving Father knows what truly is best for you, and you must choose to worship Him with total obedience above all else.

Your heart is not your friend because it is **deceitful above all things** (Jeremiah 17:9); therefore, you cannot trust your own desires, feelings, and standards. So if you cannot trust your own judgment of truth, from where should you get your truth? Psalm 119:160 states: **The sum of Your word is truth, and every one of Your righteous rules endures forever.** This is where consistent Bible study and scripture memory are paramount. If you are seeking to renew your mind by taking captive your sinful, deceitful thoughts and replacing them with God-pleasing, truthful ones, you must diligently study your Source of truth! You must know God's Word inside and out. This will help you to identify which thoughts are truthful and which are untrue. In the process, you will also be arming yourself with Biblical thoughts to dwell on instead!

Psalm 15:1-2 says: **O LORD, who shall sojourn in Your tent? Who shall dwell on Your holy hill? He who walks blamelessly and does what is right and speaks truth in his heart.** God is holy and true, and He does not tolerate lies and deceit, even in your heart! Take a moment to create a personal "thou shalt not" list of commandments you have set up for yourself. Beside each commandment, write the underlying lie or belief that each standard demonstrates. Then, write what the Word of God says instead. Below is an example of this helpful exercise, and possible lies those struggling with an eating disorder may believe:

MY STANDARD	WHAT LIE AM I BELIEVING?	WHAT DOES THE BIBLE SAY?
I shall not gain above a certain weight.	I will be content if people accept me.	Galatians 1:10: I should be seeking the approval of God, not others. Philippians 4:12-13: Contentment comes through Christ, not gratifying my desires.

I shall not eat bread.	I must do everything I can to not gain weight. I will be happy if I stay thin.	2 Corinthians 5:9: Being thin is not my ultimate goal. Psalm 1: True joy comes not with being thin, but with delighting in God and His Word.
I shall not limit my food intake when I've had a hard day.	Eating calms my anxiety. I deserve to eat whatever I want when I've had a hard day.	1 Corinthians 6:19-20: My body is not mine to do as I please. Isaiah 26:3: Perfect peace comes from fixing my mind on Christ!

Now you have a tool to help you when you are tempted to believe lies. Pull out your list of standards and direct your thinking on the truth you have found in the Word of God! This is a great step in demolishing the enslaving lies of an eating disorder. Renewing your mind is not an easy feat, and it takes a lifetime of hard work to renew your thought life, but this is what your loving Father is calling you to do! This is something you cannot accomplish in your own strength, but it becomes a beautiful opportunity to cry out to the Lord for help. When you become discouraged, take heart and remember 2 Peter 1:3: **His divine power has granted to us all things that pertain to life and godliness, through the knowledge of him who called us to his own glory and excellence.** If you are a true child of God, then you have the powerful Spirit of God dwelling in you to help you live a godly life. Don't minimize His power. Strive to know Him more and more, and persevere by His awesome might!

Speaking the Truth in Love

A second part of mind renewal is **speaking the truth in love** from Ephesians 4:15. 1 Corinthians 13:1-8a presents a detailed idea of what love looks like:

> **If I speak in the tongues of men and of angels, but have not love, I am a noisy gong or a clanging cymbal. ² And if I have prophetic powers, and understand all mysteries and all knowledge, and if I have all faith, so as to remove mountains, but have not love, I am nothing. ³ If I give away all I have, and if I deliver up my body to be burned, but have not love, I gain nothing. ⁴ Love is patient and kind; love does not envy or boast; it is not arrogant ⁵ or rude. It does not insist on its own way; it is not irritable or resentful; ⁶ it does not rejoice at wrongdoing, but rejoices with the truth. ⁷ Love bears all things, believes all things, hopes all things, endures all things. ⁸ Love never ends.**

In this passage, God first establishes the importance of love. He says that anything a person does or says without love is meaningless (verses 1-3). Then, God lays down what real love is supposed to look like: love is patient, kind, selfless, trusting, hoping, persevering, humble, unfailing, taking no delight in evil, and rejoicing in the truth (verses 4-8a). As you learn to speak truth to yourself, you will need to return to this "love list" often to compare how your speech aligns with God's description.

As shown in the verses above, speaking truth to yourself does not mean telling yourself only what you want to hear.

Minimizing or justifying the problem would not be rejoicing in the truth, would not be humble, and would certainly not be selfless. On the other hand, speaking truth in love doesn't mean incessantly repeating your failures to yourself, since that would be unkind and appear to be taking delight in evil. Neither of the above extremes captures the biblical idea of speaking the truth in love. So, what does speaking the truth in love actually look like? How can it be applied to disordered eating and used to replace lies with truth? Let's return to our list of lies from chapter 2 and address the first three lies in detail below:

1) **Beauty**: *In today's world*, beauty is primarily about appearance. *In today's world*, beauty is a goal: something a person strives to achieve or to possess. Beauty can be very expensive, a god requiring the sacrifice of obscene amounts of time and money before delivering. *In today's world*, beauty doesn't last forever.

   In God's Word, beauty is more about attitude than appearance. *In God's Word*, physical beauty is shown as the cheap substitute for what God considers true, unfading beauty. While physical beauty concerns itself with capturing another's heart, biblical beauty is more about capturing your own heart in reverence to the Lord. Unlike the world's beauty, the beauty that God cares about comes from a beautiful heart that fears the LORD (Proverbs 31:30). In 1 Peter, a woman with **"imperishable beauty"** is described as possessing **"a gentle and quiet spirit, which in God's sight is very precious"** (1 Peter 3:4).

   In God's Word, beauty is not the end goal. Rather, the goal is to reflect the beauty of God's Son, Jesus, to the world. Paul writes to the Corinthians that **we all,**

with unveiled face, behold the glory of the Lord [and] are being transformed into the same image from one degree of glory to another (2 Corinthians 3:18). When the Bible talks about "glory," it means majesty and splendor of character. When you "glorify" God, it means you are acting in accordance with His splendid character. Glorifying God is not only your life's purpose, but it was also Jesus' purpose when He was on earth. Jesus was all about reflecting His Father, God, to the world, so that the people could know God (Hebrews 1:3 and Matthew 11:27).

Reflecting Christ's beauty to the world is paramount: this world is searching, but it does not know what true beauty looks like. True beauty is about beholding and revealing the beauty of Jesus Christ: the beauty of a Holy God who gave up everything for the chance at a relationship with the world, with you. As you behold His beauty, you bear it to the world and represent what Christ would look like. This is what it means to be beautiful, according to the Bible. To combat the lies of beauty in your life, ask yourself, "Whose beauty am I reflecting, God's or my own?"

2) **Perfectionism and Performance**: Acceptance is a major motivator of human behavior, along with its antonym: rejection. One of the ways you might try and obtain acceptance is through performance. As an association between performance and acceptance is strengthened, so is an association between failure and rejection. Better performance becomes your main goal, and perfectionism becomes an increasingly common self-expectation.

Disordered eating offers a variety of solutions to the problem of imperfection: Perhaps as a way to punish yourself for missing perfection, perhaps to prove you can be good at something, perhaps as a means to appear as close to perfections as possible, and so on. Enter, forgiveness.

As it turns out, the perfect body cannot solve your feelings of worthlessness because eating disorders are a distortion of the spirit, as well as of the body. Feelings of deep shame often plant themselves in the souls of individuals with eating disorders, creating "problem areas" below the skin: wimpy personalties, wrinkly hearts, ugly minds, obese needs.

If you loathe your body for its imperfections, forgiveness offers freedom that was previously unattainable. As you carry your failures to the cross, Jesus reminds you that He never intended for you to be perfect. He reminds you that He not only forgives you for your imperfections, but in fact designed them. God gets great glory in your imperfection, and you get great grace. God was well aware of this when he said in 2 Corinthians 12:9: **My grace is sufficient for you, for my power is made perfect in weakness.** Again, in Isaiah 29:19: **the humble will rejoice in the LORD; the needy will rejoice in the Holy One of Israel.**

Finally, the Bible assures you the only person capable of perfection is Christ, and you are counted "perfect" by association. 2 Corinthians 5:21 says it this way: **For our sake he made him to be sin who knew no sin, so that in him we might become the righteousness of God.**

Instead of performance and perfection, this is what will mark your life as valuable and successful: you boast in your weaknesses and humbly rejoice in Christ's perfection.

3) **Control**: Have you ever found yourself getting anxious because your life seemed uncontrollable? Have you ever tried to control something, and ended up with chaos? Have you ever relinquished control when you really should have taken it? The lies of "I must be in control," "I can't control anything," and "my life is out of control" are paralyzing when you are struggling with destructive eating habits.

Take binging and purging habits, for example. You may decide to binge when you become overwhelmed by a life circumstance. During the binge, you may feel out of control. After binging, you may regain a sense of control by purging. Binging laments that life is out of control, and purging puts you in control. Where is God in the midst of this chaos? Why is knowing and believing God's control (what the Bible calls "sovereignty") so important in winning the victory over destructive eating? Can you have peace in a seemingly uncontrollable world?

"God is in control, you are not in control." That simple statement is the key to understanding and accepting God's gift of sovereignty to you. The word "sovereign" is used of God to describe His indisputable and total control over all the affairs of the world. From the forces of nature, to the decisions of persons, to the turning of tables, to the speed and direction of growing mildew! Yes, the Bible is no stranger to God's mighty control over the universe. In 1 Chronicles 29:11-12, you read about God's ability to strengthen and establish people and places: **Yours, O Lord, is the greatness and the power and the glory and the victory and the majesty, for all that is in the heavens and in the earth is yours. Yours is the kingdom, O Lord, and you are exalted as head above all. Both riches and honor come from you, and you rule over all. In your hand are power and might, and in your hand it is to make great and to give strength to all.**

In Proverbs, you can learn that even "chance" and "accidents" are ultimately God's decisions (16:33). What God decides to do, He does, and no one can do anything unless God wants it to happen (Job 23:13; Psalm 135:6; Isaiah 14:27; and Lamentations 3:37, for starters). God's complete control is not meant to smother you. Rather, the Bible says that God is in control to provide you peace. Colossians 3:15 says you are called to **let the peace of God RULE** in your heart. Control and peace are directly correlated: your mind is at rest as you trust the God who is good, cares for you, and controls everything. Psalm 4:8 draws out this point further by relating rest and sleep to your confidence in God's control: **In peace I will both lie down and sleep; for You alone, O Lord, make me dwell in safety.** In addition, God's control gives you the ammunition to combat self-inflation, as well as self-pity. God, who is in control and good, has created you. The Bible remarks that you are in no place to question why God created you one way or another (Romans 9:20). Instead, you can be confident that **God is good and does only good**; He has fashioned you intimately and intricately; He has created you for a unique purpose (Psalm 119:68, 73, Psalm 139:13-16, and Ephesians 2:10).

New Attitudes

As you identify and destroy the lies you've believed about yourself, your body, and your purpose; take this diagram as a visual of what it looks like to implement the steps of replacing lies with truth. Add to this diagram your own lies and do the hard work of replacing them with God's truth. Hear the chains fall off and walk in freedom!

Lie	Truth	Proof
1) **Be Beautiful**: *I am only as valuable as I am beautiful. Beauty equals happiness. No one will like me if I'm ugly. I won't get married unless my body is up to par. Skinny = Happy. Beautiful people always get what they want.*	**Be a Reflection of Christ's Beauty**	Proverbs 31:30 2 Corinthians 3:18 2 Corinthians 4:6-18 Isaiah 52:7 Matthew 23:27 Ephesians 5:1 1 Peter 3:3-4
2) **Be Perfect**: *Failure is ugly and unacceptable. Failure displeases God. Other people may fail, but that's not an option for me. I must appear to have everything together. I must be perfect.*	**Be Forgiven**	Luke 5:23-24 Luke 17:3-4 1 John 1:8 10 Ephesians 1:7 Galatians 2:20 Colossians 1:14 1 Corinthians 5:20

3) **Be in Control**: *Everything in my life is falling apart. I need to control my weight, my food intake, a number on a scale, etc.... I can't control (my weight, my food intake, my fitness, my body, etc...*	**Be at Peace**	Luke 10.6 John 14:27 Acts 10:36 Romans 15:13 Philippians 4:7 Colossians 3:15
4) **Be Comfortable**: *I cannot stand this much pain. I must avoid hard things.*	**Be Refined**	James 1: 2-5 Romans 5:3 Psalm 119: 65-72 Philippians 3:7-11 1 Corinthians 10:13 2 Corinthians 12:8-10 Lamentations 3:32-33 Job 23:10 2 Corinthians 1:3-10 2 Corinthians 4:5
5) **Be Successful**: *My goal in life is to take up as little space as possible. My goal in life is to never get fat.*	**Be a Servant**	2 Corinthians 5:9 1 Corinthians 10:31 Colossians 1:10-11 Psalm 63:1-4 Galatians 5:13-14 Micah 6:8 James 1:27 1 Thessalonians 4:1 1 Thessalonians 5:16-18 Romans 12 Deuteronomy 6:1-9 1 Peter 3:8-12

6) **Be Self-Sufficient**: *Food is my enemy. Food can only be eaten in certain circumstances and in certain ways. Everything I consume must be taken into account and logged.*	**Be Humble**	1 Timothy 4:3-5 Exodus 16:4 and 17 Matthew 6:11 Proverbs 30:8-9 Genesis 3:19 Psalm 103:14
7) **Be Skinny**: I am not healthy *until I weigh [blank]. I know my body and what's best for it is thinness.*	**Be a Steward**	1 Timothy 4:8 Romans 12:1; 6:12-13 Romans 8:13 1 Corinthians 6:13-20 2 Corinthians 7:1 1 Peter 1:13-16; 2:11-12
8) **Be Athletic**: Exercise is my *primary tool against the battle of weight gain. Exercise must be performed in relation to how much I eat.*	**Be Hard-Working**	1 Corinthians 9:24-27 Hebrews 12:1-3 James 1:12
9) **Self-imposed Rules**: If I just follow my *own set of rules, I won't get fat and others will accept me. If I eat a cookie, I just need to workout twice as long today to make up for it.*	**Be a Doer of God's Laws**	James 1:22-25 Psalm 18:22; 19:9; 22:28; 89:30; 119:7; 119:30 1 Thessalonians 4:1-3

10) **People-pleasing**: *Others will not like me unless I am beautiful. I need to look a certain way for them to accept me.*	**Be Focused upon Pleasing Christ First**	2 Corinthians 5:9-10 Galatians 1:10

KATIE'S DIARY

November 23rd

Dear Diary,

With my counselor's help, I'm identifying some lies I believe. I used to think my eating disorder would somehow diminish my problems. Like, if I were smaller my problems would be too.... I realize now that problems don't stem from an inflated body, they stem from an inflated heart! I can see now that in trying to take control, I was pridefully dethroning God. I was sitting on His lap, pretending that I was calling the shots! Knowing how quick I am to "play God," I've had to radically amputate some of my "go-to" attitudes and actions. For instance, I don't allow myself to change in front of mirrors anymore. Not that mirrors are evil, I just know for me, where I'm at right now, it's not good to spend a lot of time in front of them. My main goal is to reflect God, not myself!

XO, Katie

Chapter Four
Walking in Victory

Know this: God wants you to be victorious for His own glory. In the first step of biblical change, He provides you with a Savior. He provides you with a picture of victory in His Son, Jesus Christ, who suffered immeasurable anguish but did so willingly for the greater good: salvation to those who repent and trust in Him alone for the forgiveness of sin. Likewise, you may have to suffer at first as you learn to sacrifice what is comfortable and familiar in the second step of change called *putting-off*. In addition, you may have to battle your own thinking when you believe lies rather than God's truth.

In a sense, you could be your own worst enemy, so mind renewal is the third step in the process of change. Jeremiah 17:9 states: **The heart is deceitful above all things, and desperately sick; who can understand it?** If the heart is more deceitful than anything else, then we have no hope in "following our hearts" as some say in worldly circles. Our own hearts deceive us above all other things! So we are told by God to follow His Word and to renew our minds and hearts with truth and new desires. The Holy Spirit working in partnership with God's Word enables us to have new desires (Philippians 2:12b-13) causing us to walk in the works God has ordained for us (Ephesians 2:10).

Thankfully, Christ is a picture of freedom and newness of life. You have a *visible* goal in Jesus as revealed in the Holy Scriptures. God wants you to progressively become like Him according to Ephesians 4:24, which is the final and fourth step in the process of change: **and to put on the new self, created**

after the likeness of God in true righteousness and holiness. 2 Timothy 3:16 refers to this part of the process of biblical change as **training in righteousness.** It is the doing of the third correction step and results in not going back to slavery. This fourth step fills the hunger void with true righteousness and holiness which is what Jesus is calling us to pursue. In this chapter, you will discover your true motivation for overcoming an eating disorder and what a triumphant life looks like.

Biblical Process for Change

	Step 1	Step 2	Step 3	**Step 4**
Ephesians 4:20-24	Learned Christ (v. 20-21)	Put-Off (v. 22)	Renewed in the Spirit of Your Mind (v. 23)	**Put-On (v. 24)**
2 Timothy 3:16	Doctrine	Reproof	Correction	**Instruction in Righteousness**
Explanation	Standard set by your Creator found in His Word	Falling short of that Standard, this is the part of your former life of sinful habits to be discarded	Holy Spirit provides power to transform with new attitude and new ability to please God	**Practical application of righteousness of Christ that now meets God's standard!**

Motivation

You can be sure that God is well-pleased with your desire to find freedom from your disordered eating and poor stewardship of your body in the past. This goal is one that honors the Lord, and you can be sure that He is faithful to provide what you need to complete His good work in you (Philippians 1:6). God is pleased whether you "feel" like He is pleased or not. He is pleased when your goal is to glorify Him. However, if you do not have the right motivation, it will be very easy to fall back into the very habits you are fighting to be rid of or to perform in a new way with old motivations leading to a different form of slavery.[13] How sad that would be! This next chapter is a recap of what should be your overall, greatest motivation in overcoming an eating disorder.

First and foremost, remember your goal in life. According to 2 Corinthians 5:9 and Romans 8:28-29, your goal in life is to **please God by becoming more and more like Jesus Christ.** This goal should drive everything you do, every thought you think, and every word you speak. You should constantly be asking yourself, "What would be most pleasing to God right now?" This is to be your number one, ultimate goal. God is pleased when we live for His glory and not our own.

Secondly, remember that the Bible teaches if you are a true child of God, your body is not your own. You were bought with a price, and your body is the temple of the Spirit of the living, loving God (1 Corinthians 6:19-20). You are called to be a good steward of all that God has entrusted you with (Matthew 25), including your body. This means that you are to eat and drink in a way that takes care of your body, recognizing that it is not yours to abuse. This glorifies God, showing His character with your very eating habits (1 Corinthians 10:31).

Do not be fooled by outward appearances. We know very underweight or even normal weight people who are

---

[13] For a more detailed look at your heart motives, we recommend *Love to Eat, Hate to Eat* by Elyse Fitzpatrick.

gluttons when that name is defined biblically because they are consumed with thoughts of food all of the time. They may appear healthy on the outside but their heart motives are more gluttonous than some obese persons. The outside, physical body is important to care for but it is not always indicative of what is going on inside a person's heart. Be satisfied with being a good steward of your physical body and knowing God is pleased with you no matter what your outward appearance may be at this stage in your life.

Lastly, you must recognize that God is on your side in this, and He will provide a way out of every temptation you encounter (1 Corinthians 10:13). You no longer have the excuse of "I can't help it," "That's just the way I am," or "It's too hard!" You must choose to believe the words of Jesus when He said: **You will receive *power* when the Holy Spirit has come upon you** (Acts 1:8). Don't forget that the God whose arm is **not too short to save, nor his ears too dull to hear** (Isaiah 59:1) is the very same God whose powerful Spirit dwells within you if you are His child. When you are tempted to accept a defeated feeling, remember that Jesus in His mercy has already won the battle for you (John 16:33). Run to God's Word and remember who He is. (For a great reminder, see Job 38-42).

God is in the business of redeeming broken people. By God's grace, you can live in victory; not only for a week, or month, or even a year, but for the rest of your life![14]

---

[14] For a more detailed, in-depth look at eating disorders, we recommend *Redeemed from the Pit* by Marie Notcheva.

KATIE'S DIARY

December 17th

Dear Diary,

Life is really SUPER hard around the holidays (and food) and all . . . I know my life's purpose is to glorify God and to please Him in everything I do, but I can't honestly say I've been perfect. At the same time, I know now that I'm not meant to be perfect. God's the perfect one, not me. I know that when I mess up (because I do) God doesn't condemn me. I'm really praying hard that God would help me use my body to serve others this Christmas season. Oh, and I realized why I hated God so much: I didn't really KNOW anything about who God really was. I made God out to be impatient, mean-spirited, distant, and selfish. Come to think of it, that sounds a lot more like me than God . . . The God I hated was not the true God, He was my (mis)understanding of God. My counseling and personal time in God's Word have helped me come to know and love the true God, not some made-up version of Him. Oh, gotta go now . . . dinner's on the table. God, please give me the grace to glorify you "whether I eat or drink or whatever I do." Amen.

XO, Katie

Chapter Five
A Triumphant Life

January 5th

Dear Diary,

I can't believe it's been a year since I moved out of my parent's house... SO crazy, right? Currently, I'm living with a family from the church that I started going to back in September. Don't laugh, but I actually look forward to attending church every week... and I go to Bible study, too. I know, I know... I never thought I'd EVER be at this point in my life. I honestly thought my life was irredeemable, unfixable. I couldn't have been more wrong! I'm so thankful for people who give me a chance and show me how much they love me (like the family I live with, and my counselor, and my bible study group). More than that, I'm thankful for people who point me to God. He gives me more chances and love than anyone on this earth ever will. It's a miracle, really. I have another miracle for you, if you're interested. I've been writing my parents! It started out as an assignment my biblical counselor gave me to ask their forgiveness for some things. I'm really hopeful God can help me reconnect with them. If anyone can help, He can!

XO, Katie

KATIE'S DIARY

February 14th

Dear Diary,

It's Valentine's day (go figure). I am wrestling with my thoughts about Josh today... I know it's been a long time since he's even talked to me...he probably doesn't even remember me. I got a box of chocolates from my parents today (yes, the people who HAVE to love me ... Does it get any lonelier?) I know they're just trying to make me feel loved. And in reality, I AM loved. I know my parents love me, but more than that I know my Heavenly Father loves me! He tells me so, every day. Maybe not in the way I feel, or the circumstances I'm in. But God died on the cross for me, and that's really the most loving thing anyone has ever done for me, ya know? I don't want to get all gruesome about it, or gushy. I'm not interested in sentiments, but I do need truth. If I don't take my thoughts captive, I will fail. Next to me, I have that box of chocolates . . . I bet I could scarf and barf them in under an hour . . . Next to my box of chocolates, I have my verse cards. I'm working through 1 Corinthians 13:4-8, Romans 5:8, 1 John 3:1, and Psalm 107:9. I know victory is impossible on my own, but God's Spirit in me is helping me in this weakness and it's not up to me to be strong but to rely on His strength in me (I got that little nugget from Romans 8:26-27). You go, God!

XO, Katie

KATIE'S DIARY

March 6th

Dear Diary,

I have crossed several milestones in the last year and a half. I've taken some terrible, awful, no good, very bad steps backward. By God's grace, I've also taken some amazing, awesome, so good, very rad leaps forward! I'm no longer going to individual counseling; my parents have agreed to start coming with me! There's been a lot of progress in that relationship, but there's still a ton to go. I've also seen progress in how I handle my body, weight, and food. I've been able to establish a routine for regular exercise, but I log how much I'm doing and I show this to my accountability partner. I have a similar routine of accountability for my food intake.

XO, Katie

KATIE'S DIARY

April 1st

Dear Diary,

At this point, denial and pride are my biggest enemies. It's so easy for me to deny I ever had a problem. It's a slippery slope, really. After all, if I don't have a problem, then I don't need safeguards. And if I don't have safeguards, I don't need others prodding into my affairs. And if I don't have others prodding into my affairs, I don't need to talk to anyone. And if I don't talk to anyone, I become a very private and secretive person . . . not really the place I want to be! As I learn to live a victorious life, I cannot keep secrets, living in darkness and concealing my affairs. I can pretend God doesn't know what's going on . . . but He does. I know it's going to be hard for me to keep living for God's beauty rather than my own. I know it's going to be hard to surrender control (that I don't really have anyway, right?). I know I'm going to fail (but God remains faithful). In the midst of all the battles, God has never given me reason to return to my old life. He is renewing me, day by day, to look more like Him. Though outwardly I struggle and fail and fade and die, He breathes life into my dead, dry bones. He puts a new heart in me, and He sets it to beating, at His beck and call. He turns everything in my life into an opportunity for good and glory. He goes ahead of me. He walks with me. He holds me. He never leaves me. He fights for me. And He wins.

XO, Katie

CONCLUSION

As you continue on your fight to have victory over your sin, remember that it is God who does the most work. He acts on your behalf, and He gives you the motivation to act yourself (Philippians 2:12b-13). Ask Him to give you the "desire to" and the "ability to" have victory over your sin. God is in the business of freeing captives, and He won't stop now: He has a mind to set you free as you surrender to Him.

Every time you hunger and thirst, remember that Jesus has offered himself as satisfaction. He says: **If anyone is thirsty, let him come and drink** (John 7:37-39) and **he who drinks of the water I give him will never thirst again** (John 4:13-14). All people hunger. All people seek to be satisfied. Unfortunately, many people spend a lifetime pursuing the things of this world, only to find out at the end of their lives that this world can't satisfy. Why? Why do people clamor after sex, drugs, control, food, etc? What is so uncomfortable about emptiness? It comes back to God's design: All people are designed to find satisfaction fully in Christ. What the world has to offer might temporarily bring happiness, but will ultimately yield a desire for more.

Instead of hungering for idolatrous desires that produce confusion, guilt, and shame, the Lord wants you to hunger for that which He desires for you. God's will requires you to make hard choices on the front end, but leads to ultimate satisfaction in Him. This is why hunger—whether physical, emotional, or otherwise—is an act of God's grace and love toward you. God allows you to experience emptiness and longing now, only to remind you that He has a better plan in mind for you, one that includes complete joy and pleasure as you glorify Him, and ultimately worship Him in heaven (see Psalm 16:11 and John 15:11). Do not "go it alone": find a trusted Christian friend or three of them to encourage you along the way. Keep fighting the good fight of faith, and experience God's love poured out and available in abundance to you. Redemption and progressively becoming like Christ is true beauty that comes from within.

APPENDIX A
WORLDLY WORDS VS. GOD'S WORD

Worldly Word	God's Word	Scripture
Addiction	Enslaving Desire	Romans 6; James 1:14-15 Proverbs 5:22
Binging	Gluttony	Proverbs 23:20-21 Philippians 3:18-19 Psalm 78:18 Proverbs 5:23
Depression	Despair	Jonah 4; Psalm 13 Genesis 4:3-7 Lamentations 3:19-26
Eating Disorder	Poor Stewardship	1 Corinthians 6:19-20 Romans 12:1 1 Corinthians 10:31 Matthew 25`
Sexy	Harlot	Proverbs 5:1-6 Proverbs 7
Independence	Rebellious	Proverbs 14:12 1 Samuel 15:22-23 Deuteronomy 28:47-48
Insecurity	Fear of Man	1 Peter 2:9; Genesis 1:27 2 Corinthians 5:17 Galatians 3:27-29
Manipulation	Deceit	Matthew 7:15 2 Corinthians 11:14 Judges 16
Perfectionist	Deccived	1 John 1:8 Psalm 119:96 Romans 3:23
Popularity	Self-Worship	Luke 14:7-14 James 2:7-13 John 15:18-25 Ezekiel 28:17 Matthew 6
Rebel	Fool	Proverbs 1:7; 12:15 Proverbs 13:10; 28:26
Self-Esteem	Pride	2 Corinthians 3:1-6 2 Corinthians 10:12-18 Proverbs 29:23 1 Peter 5:6

Books and Booklets by Mark Shaw

<u>Books</u>

The Heart of Addiction
    Workbook
        Leader's Guide
Relapse: Biblical Prevention Strategies
Divine Intervention: Hope and Help for Families of Addicts
Addiction-Proof Parenting
Cross Talking: A Daily Gospel for Transforming Addicts
Eating Disorders: Help for Hungering Souls
Strength in Numbers: The Team Approach to Biblical Counseling

<u>Booklets</u>

Hope and Help through Biblical Counseling
Hope and Help for Sexual Temptation
Hope and Help for Gambling
Hope and Help for Self-Injurers and Cutters
Hope and Help for Marriage
Hope and Help for Husbands and Fathers
Hope and Help for Video Game, TV, Internet "Addiction"
The Pursuit of Perfection (with William Hines)
Understanding Temptation: The War Within Your Heart

www.focuspublishing.com